CW00589736

It's never too late ...
to sing

A teach-yourself tutor with interactive CD

HEIDI PEGLER &
PAM WEDGWOOD

© 2011 by Faber Music Ltd
This edition first published in 2011 by Faber Music Ltd
Bloomsbury House 74–77 Great Russell Street London WC1B 3DA
Music processed by Jackie Leigh
Text designed by Susan Clarke
Cover design by Lydia Merrills-Ashcroft
CD recorded and produced by Oliver Wedgwood
Printed in England by Caligraving Ltd
All rights reserved

ISBN10: 0-571-53432-5
EAN13: 978-0-571-53432-6

To buy Faber Music publications or to find out about the full range of titles available
please contact your local music retailer or Faber Music sales enquiries:
Faber Music Ltd, Burnt Mill, Elizabeth Way, Harlow CM20 2HX
Tel: +44 (0) 1279 82 89 82   Fax: +44 (0) 1279 82 89 83
sales@fabermusic.com   fabermusicstore.com

Foreword

Everyone has the ability to sing, and the aim of this book is to help you discover your own unique voice. As you work through the units try not to copy other singers but explore and develop your own sound instead.

This book is intended for anyone who hasn't had lessons before or who has a limited amount of knowledge. You don't need to read music but as you progress you may start to recognise notes and rhythmic patterns.

The accompanying CD contains all the exercises and songs. The exercises are demonstrated by a singer, and the songs contain the vocal line played by an instrumental sound where necessary to help you follow your part and sing along.

Practising your singing

At the start you should aim to sing for about 15–20 minutes at a time but as you progress and your voice gets stronger you may like to do more than one session a day. Sing at a comfortable volume and if the voice gets tired, then stop. If there are any signs of strain or stress (such as a sore throat), stop the session and resume at a later time. If these signs keep occurring then seek advice from a singing teacher.

Try to think about what you are doing rather than re-enforcing old singing habits. Find a room to sing where you are free from distractions and inhibitions. As you become more confident you may like to record yourself so you can listen objectively. Keep notes about the new singing sensations that you discover.

This book can be used without a singing teacher but if you want to learn more and progress at a faster pace then a teacher is highly recommended. There is more information about how to find a good singing teacher on page 79.

Singing is really a simple process which can become confused and clouded in mystery. This book sets out the basic principles of technique at the same time as learning how to communicate a message and express emotion. Have fun!

How to use the book

This book is split into progressive units, with the main learning point of each section shown in the box in the top corner. You will find information in *Top tips* and new points of music theory are introduced in the *Reading the dots* boxes. You will see the CD symbols by the songs and exercises:

1 = CD track number. Exercises are introduced with your first note and a count-in. All the songs begin with a piano introduction which is shown in small notes.

The *It's Never Too Late to Sing Piano Accompaniments* book (0-571-53669-7) contains the accompaniments to all the exercises and songs, or they are available to download from *fabermusicstore.com*.

Reading music

If you play an instrument – or if you learnt music a long time ago – you may not need to work through everything on this page. However, you may like to use it for revision!

Feeling the beat

Just as you have a regular heartbeat, music has a regular beat (or pulse) too. Note and rest values are defined by a number of beats or counts:

Note and rest values					
𝅝	=	semibreve or whole note*	=	4 counts	▬
𝅗𝅥	=	minim or half note	=	2 counts	▬
♩	=	crotchet or quarter note	=	1 count	𝄽
♪	=	quaver or eighth note	=	½ count	𝄾
𝅘𝅥𝅯	=	semiquaver or sixteenth note	=	¼ count	𝄿

Notes are grouped into **bars** (measures) by **barlines**. At the end of a piece there is a **double barline**. If the double barline has two dots before it, this is a repeat sign and instructs you to return to the beginning of the piece or section.

Time signatures

These appear at the beginning of a piece of music and tell you how many beats or counts there are in each bar (or measure). The top figure tells you the number of beats in each bar; the bottom figure tells you the value of those beats.

4/4 = 4 x ♩ counts in each bar		**2/4** = 2 x ♩ counts in each bar
3/4 = 3 x ♩ counts in each bar		▬ = whole-bar rest for any time signature

All about pitch

To show their pitch, notes are written on a five-line stave.
Notes are written on the lines or in the spaces:

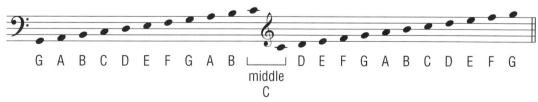

Each stave has a **clef** at the beginning to fix the pitch of the notes. For high notes we use the **treble clef** (𝄞); for low notes we use the **bass clef** (𝄢). Solo vocal music is traditionally written in the treble clef irrespective of whether the voice is high (female) or low (male). The male voice will automatically sing the notes an octave lower than written (see *Classify your voice* on page 40 for more information on this).

* English followed by US terms are given throughout.

Getting started

Posture and alignment

Your whole body is involved in producing the sound when you sing, so it's important that your body helps you perform to the best of your ability. You need an upright posture that is relaxed and open, so the breath can flow in and out effortlessly. The **feet** should be planted firmly on the floor about a shoulder width apart with your weight evenly distributed. The **knees** need to be relaxed and not locked. The **chest** has a feeling of openness with the arms hanging loosely at the sides. The **shoulders** are relaxed and down and the **head** and **neck** area should feel free of any unhelpful tension. Sometimes we are unaware of this tension – try these exercises in front of a full length mirror so you can observe the changes in your posture:

Stretching

Stretch your right arm above the head and lean over to the left. Feel a stretch in the muscles around your rib cage. Repeat this with the other arm then stretch both arms up and clasp the hands together. Open your arms out, bringing them down slowly. The rib cage should feel more open and higher than before.

Rolling down and up

Stand with your feet shoulder-width apart and your knees slightly bent (not locked). Gently allow your upper body to drop forwards as if you were about to touch your toes (like a rag doll). Your head and arms should hang towards the floor and you should be looking at your knees! Don't worry if you can't get all the way down. In this position, think about releasing any tension in the neck and gently shake your shoulders. Breathe deeply and notice the expansion in the lower back as you inhale. Very slowly, roll up until you are in a standing position, imagining each vertebra moving back into place as you unwind. When you have returned to a standing position, roll your shoulders to release any tension.

Should I stand or sit when I am singing?

It is always best to stand when you are singing as it is easier to breathe and the whole body can give support to the voice. However, choristers often sit during a long rehearsal. Make sure you sit forward on your chair with your feet flat on the floor: don't slump back or perch too far forward.

top tip Do not cross your legs when you are sitting and singing – it will inhibit your breathing!

As singers, we need to get the correct balance between muscular tension and relaxation. In order to do this we may have to rid our bodies of bad postural habits or unhelpful tension. A teacher can help you further with this as they can watch for any signs of tension when you are singing.

Breathing: the power supply

Breathing is obviously important for singing but can often become clouded in mystery and terminology. Breathing for singing is an extension of what we are doing naturally every day in order to stay alive.

- Lie on the floor with a book placed under your head. Place one hand on your rib cage and one on your lower abdomen. What do you notice? Observe your breathing pattern.

- When you breathe in, the rib cage and the lower abdomen move out and as you let the air out they return. Watch your lower abdomen go up and down and listen to the breathing pattern of your body.

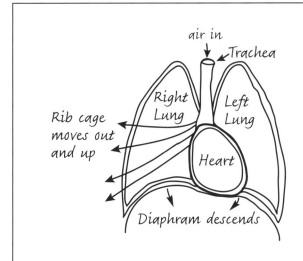

The science of breathing

The diaphragm is shaped like a parachute and is a large, dome-shaped layer of muscle. It is situated just under the rib cage and helps in the breathing process. As you breathe in, the ribs move out and up and the diaphragm tightens and lowers, creating a vacuum in the lungs which expand as they fill with air. At the same time the lower abdominal area is pushed out slightly (which explains why it is uncomfortable to sing after a big meal!). As you let the air out, the diaphragm relaxes upwards and the rib muscles relax, which in turn help the lungs send out the air.

top tip When you breathe in, the rib and abdominal area expands and when you breathe out the rib and abdominal area contracts. Sometimes this can be confused so that the opposite is happening!

Try this

You can do this exercise lying down on the floor or standing up. Put one hand on your lower abdominal muscles (tummy area) and one hand on your lower ribs. Blow out the air. Next, breathe in deeply (through the nose is good) and feel your body expand out and round. Let the air out on an 'sss' sound making sure the 'sss' is strong and with an even intensity – you will feel the lower abdominal muscles contract/tighten. When you get to the end of the breath, relax your lower abdominal muscles and let the air in again. Repeat the process.

One of the singer's greatest fears can be running out of breath. However, it is important not to hold onto the breath or over breathe as the body and the voice can become tense and tight. Allow the breath to flow – don't save it!

unit 1

Warming up

Singing is an athletic activity for which the body needs to be ready to work to its best ability. Athletes wouldn't dream of racing before warming up and you should approach singing in the same way. It is important to work out your own warm-up routine, but here are some exercises for you to get started. First we need to think about our posture:

- Rock backwards and forwards on your feet until you find an equal balance on both feet (not too far over the toes or too far back on the heels).

- Then find the same balance with the hips and shoulders, which shouldn't be slumped or rigid.

- Lastly, think about your head: the chin should be level – not held too high or forced down too low. Imagine the crown of your head is growing upward and feel the length in your neck and spine.

Our warm-up exercises will be made up of **scales** (notes that move by step) and small jumps (**intervals**). To get used to singing a five-note scale, practise the exercise below using either the numbers or the **sol-fa** names. The CD will help and guide you.

1 2 3 4 5   5 4 3 2 1
Doh ray me fah soh,   soh fah me ray doh.

This is a repeat sig

fact file

After the clef, a **key signature** is always given, to tell you what key the song is in. In these exercises, the two ♯ (**sharps**) indicate we are in D major.

In this exercise we are going to jump over notes two and four so we are only singing notes one, three and five. This pattern has a special name – it is called the **tonic triad** and you will often hear it at a railway station or an airport before an announcement. Again, use the CD to guide you.

1 3 1 3 5   5 3 5 3 1
Doh me doh me soh,   soh me soh me doh.

You may remember the French song, *Frère Jacques*. It is made up of steps and small jumps. Sing this song and try following the pattern of the music at the same time:

1 2 3 1   1 2 3 1   3 4 5   3 4 5
Frè - re Jac - ques, Frè - re Jac - ques, Dor - mez vous? Dor - mez vous?

5 6 5 4 3 1   5 6 5 4 3 1   1 5 1   1 5 1
Son - nez les ma - ti - nes, Son - nez les ma - ti - nes, Ding, dang, dong! Ding, dang, dong!

Now let's get our breathing going:

- Place your hand on your abdominal muscles. Let the air out slowly on a 'shhhh' sound, like an old steam train.

- Relax the abdominal muscles and breathe in.

- Let the air out again as before but a little faster this time.

- Keep repeating this pattern but gradually accelerating the speed of the exhalation (train). As the train gets faster the in-breaths (puffs) get shorter. Make sure the abdominal muscles are working hard for you.

Now for some gentle warm-up exercises to practise your breathing. Breathe only where there is a tick (✓) and try to get your lips to tickle on the humming line. The CD demonstrates the different vowel sounds on the repeats.

top tip This exercise gets higher every time you repeat it.

Hmm____	hmm____	hmm_____
Moo____	moo____	moo_____
Mee____	mee____	mee_____
Mah____	mah____	mah_____
Moh____	moh____	moh_____

Make sure you sing this gentle running exercise in one breath. We repeat it at different pitches – as indicated on the CD:

Me_____ ah_____

For this one, hum the first bar, then use a clear 'ah' sound as you descend. Notice the jumps in the first bar, and descending scale in the 2nd and 3rd bars.

Hmm_____ ah_____

Now sing this descending five-note scale slowly and steadily:

You you you you you, blue blue blue blue blue.

Reading the dots

✓ = where to breathe

____ = an extension line after a word shows how many notes you sing to a word or syllable.

Now you are ready to sing your first song. Can you spot when the music moves by step or by a jump? This song is sung at a bouncy **tempo** (speed). Try to breathe only at the places marked with a tick. This will keep the music moving along and ensures you don't breathe in the middle of a word!

All about piano introductions

All the songs start with a piano introduction, which are shown in the music in small notes for you to follow but not sing. This will help you know when to start singing, as well as helping you find the first note you sing. Here, the introduction finishes on the first note you sing.

CD 1

When the saints go marching in

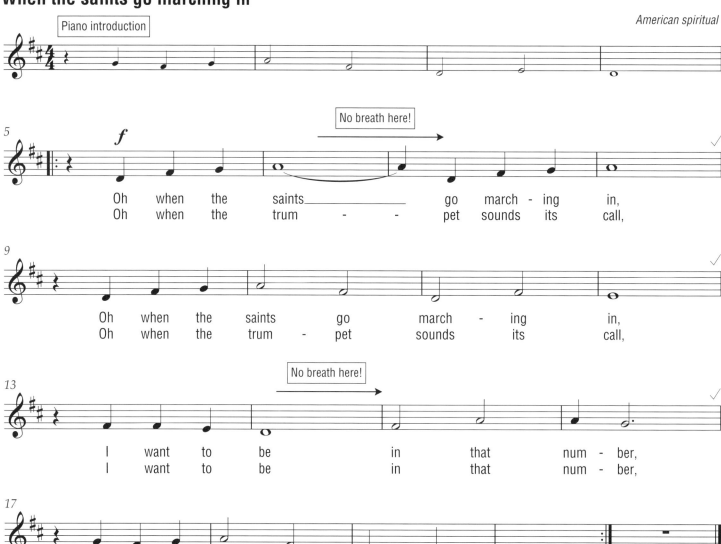

American spiritual

Oh when the saints   go march - ing in,
Oh when the trum - - pet sounds its call,

Oh when the saints go march - ing in,
Oh when the trum - pet sounds its call,

I want to be in that num - ber,
I want to be in that num - ber,

Oh when the saints go march - ing in.
Oh when the trum - pet sounds its call.

Reading the dots

4/4 = the **time signature** shows are are 4 x ♩ beats in each bar.

ƒ = **forte** = sing loudly.

5 = The small numbers given at the start of the 2nd line of music onwards are **bar numbers**. They are there to help you find places in the music quickly and easily.

'Trum - - - pet' = hyphens are added when a word is split.

Cockles and mussels

Here is another famous song for you to try. Again, try to breathe only where there is a tick. Watch out for places where you might breathe accidently and see if you can keep going! Try singing the sad last verse very softly.

Reading the dots

$\frac{3}{4}$ = the **time signature** shows there are 3 x ♩ beats in each bar.

♭ = the **key signature** of one ♭ (**flat**) shows we are in F major.

mf = *mezzo forte* = sing quite loudly.

pp = *pianissimo* = sing very softly.

⌣ = **slur** – links two or more notes, to be sung to one syllable or word.

unit 2

The tongue is a mass of muscles covered by mucous membrane and it is bigger than you think! You often hear singers referring to three areas of the tongue: the tip, the blade (middle) and the back. The tongue is crucial in singing because it helps to shape vowels and consonants and affects the sound you make. It is vital that it is flexible and free of any unnecessary tension.

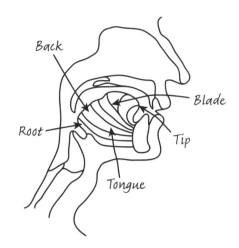

Observation

Close your eyes and try to feel where your tongue is inside your mouth. Is it flat? Is it high? Where is the tip? Use the tip of your tongue to explore your mouth. Can you make a map of your mouth in your mind?

Freeing tension in the tongue

- Look in a mirror. Place the tongue tip just behind your lower teeth, drop your jaw and push your tongue forward so that the body of it protrudes out of your mouth. Move your tongue in and out, making sure the tongue moves independently of the jaw and the tip remains behind the teeth.

- Drop your jaw and stick out your tongue as far as it will go. Now say 'the theory of relativity is nonsensical to traditional mathematicians'! Make sure the words are still clear without your tongue being involved.

The five vowels: ah, eh, ee, oh and oo

Open your mouth in an oval shape and say the vowels 'ah, eh and ee'. Make sure the tip of your tongue remains behind your bottom teeth. How does the tongue move to change each vowel sound? It is fairly flat for 'ah' and moves up and forward as you change to 'eh' and 'ee'. Now allow your lips to round as you say 'oh' and 'oo'. Practise this a few times, making sure your tongue is working and your jaw is doing as little as possible.

Now let's sing the five vowels:

To sing well, your jaw must be relaxed. As it is closely connected to the tongue and **larynx** it's essential that it's not tense and doesn't get involved when it doesn't need to. For example, the jaw shouldn't get too involved with enunciation – allow your tongue to do the work instead!

top tip You may need to check this in the mirror!

Use your tongue to make these consonants:

CD 1
11

Da	da	da	da	da	da	da	da	da	da	da	da	da	da	da	da	da
Ta	ta	ta	ta	ta	ta	ta	ta	ta	ta	ta	ta	ta	ta	ta	ta	ta
Ga	ga	ga	ga	ga	ga	ga	ga	ga	ga	ga	ga	ga	ga	ga	ga	ga
La	la	la	la	la	la	la	la	la	la	la	la	la	la	la	la	la

As we sing higher, the jaw naturally lowers a little. Don't let it open too wide at the front as this can cause tension and close the back of the throat. Instead, imagine there is a wide space at the back of the mouth (open your back teeth!). Try these ideas:

- Place the tips of your index fingers on either side of your head just in front of your ears and place your thumb under your jaw. Drop the jaw and you should feel tiny indentations under your index fingers. Say 'yah-yah-yah', keeping the jaw loose and the tip of your tongue behind your bottom teeth.

- Put the tip of your index finger between your teeth, slightly to the side. Don't open your mouth any further as you sing the following exercise:

CD 1
12

Ah_____   eh_____   ee_____   eh_____   ah

- As you sing this exercise move your jaw gently from side to side without changing the vowel sound:

CD 1
13

Ah   eh   ee   eh   ah

- Sing a five-note scale and when you get to the top note, pause and waggle your jaw before descending. Check the jaw doesn't thrust forward as this can cause tightness and tension.

CD 1
14

gently waggle jaw

Lah_____
Beh_____
Fee_____
Goh_____
Zoo_____

Further practice

Here are some fun ways of getting the tongue to do the work. You should practise these exercises in front of a mirror. Check your tongue is moving rather than your jaw.

The tip of your tongue should flick behind the top front teeth to sing words beginning with 't':

The two twen - ty - two train tore through the tun - nel.

Use the tip of your tongue for 'sl' and 'sn':

Six slip - pe - ry snails slid slow - ly sea - ward.

Use the tip of your tongue for 'n':

A noi - sy noise an - noys an oy - ster.

The tip of your tongue touches the gum ridge for 'l':

Lots of lit - tle Lon - don lamp - light - ers lit Lon - don's lit - tle lamps.

Reading the dots

At the start of some of these exercises there is a short bar of only one beat. These are called **upbeats**. When there is an upbeat, the final bar should be shortened by the value of the upbeat.

♩. = a dot after a note adds half as much again to its value. For now, the rhythm of the words should give you the correct rhythm.

♪♪♪ = **triplet** = sing three notes in one beat. See page 17 for more details.

The next two songs allow you to practise what you have learnt in this unit so far. Keep looking in a mirror so you can watch what you are doing.

My Lord what a morning

In this song, practise getting the tongue to flick independently from the jaw, particularly on words which begin with 'l', 'n', 'd' and 't'. For example, flick your tongue to say the 'l' of Lord.

American spiritual

Relaxed blues feel

My Lord what a morn - ing,

My Lord what a morn - ing, Oh my Lord what a morn - ing, When the

stars be - gin to fall, When the stars be - gin to fall. You'll

hear the trum - pet sound To wake the na - tions un - der - ground.

Going up a key!

Look-ing to my God's right hand When the stars be - gin to fall.

My Lord what a morn - ing, My Lord what a morn - ing, Oh my Lord what a

morn - ing, When the stars be - gin to fall, When the stars be - gin to fall.

Reading the dots

mp = *mezzo piano* = quite softly.

 = *crescendo* = getting louder.

= *decrescendo* = getting quieter.

These signs are known as hairpins.

Relaxed blues feel = a tempo description gives you information on how the song should be sung.

Amazing grace

This famous hymn by John Newton has a folk-like melody and quite a small range. Can you sing the first phrase in one breath? Think 'down' towards the top notes and keep your jaw relaxed and free. Breathe in slowly and deeply through your nose before you start.

fact file

When a passage is repeated but has a slightly different ending, we use **first** and **second time bars**. The first time through, sing all the music under the first bracket. When you sing the passage again, leave out bracket 1 and go straight to bracket 2.

unit 3

Reading rhythm

fact file

A **dot** after a note adds half as much again to that note's value.

♩. = ♩ + ♪ = 1½ beats

♩. = ♩ + ♩ = 3 beats

When you are learning to read music it's important to break it down into its two components – rhythm and pitch. Let's start with rhythm (the length of notes). Set yourself a steady beat by tapping your foot or walking around the room. Now try saying this rhythmic pattern:

Should   auld   ac - quain - tance   be   for - got...

Reading pitch

The next step is to look at the pitch (the highness or lowness of notes) and see if it moves by step or by jump. These jumps are called **intervals**. *Auld lang syne* starts with an interval of a fourth:

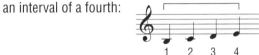

1 2 3 4

interval jump of a fourth

Should   auld   ac - quain - tance   be   for - got...

The importance of the tonic triad

In unit 1 we practised singing notes moving by step and by jumping 1, 3, 5. These three notes form the **tonic triad** of any scale. (Doh = 1, me = 3 and soh = 5.) These are the most important notes in a scale. If you can hear them clearly in your head then it is easier to jump to the other notes of the scale from them.

Practising the song

Auld lang syne contains a tonic triad going up and down – can you sing both separately from the song? The CD will help you.

CD 1
21

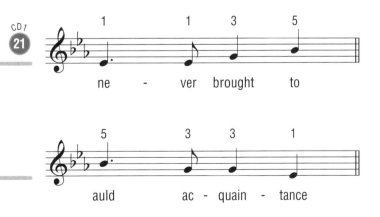

1   1   3   5

ne - ver brought to

5   3   3   1

auld   ac - quain - tance

15

Auld lang syne

'Auld lang syne' means long ago. The words were written by Robert Burns
and it is often sung at midnight on New Year's Eve.

Sentimentally ♩ = 88

Traditional

Should auld ac-quain-tance be for-got, And
here's a hand, my trust-y friend, And

ne - ver brought to mind? Should auld ac-quain-tance
gie's a hand of thine; We'll take a cup of

be for-got, And days of auld lang syne? } For auld___ lang___
kind - ness yet, For auld___ lang___ syne. }

syne my dear, For auld___ lang___ syne; We'll take a cup of

kind - ness yet For___ auld___ lang___ syne. And syne.

Reading the dots

⌣⌣ = a **dotted slur** shows that one verse needs a slur to fit the words, but the
other verse doesn't. So you don't always slur these notes.

♩ = 88 = a **metronome mark** often appears at the start of a piece. You can set this
number on a metronome to hear the **speed** of the song if you like. Here you have
88 x ♩ per minute.

When I fall in love

This song was originally sung by Doris Day in the film *One minute to zero*, but it is the version by Nat King Cole which most people remember.

Reading the dots

┌─3─┐ means that the three notes bracketed are played in same time as two. Listen to CD to get the feel of this rhythm. It is called a **triplet**.

Words by Edward Heyman
Music by Victor Young

© 1952 (renewed) Chappell & Co Inc   Warner/Chappell North America Ltd
Reproduced by permission of Alfred Publishing Co Inc for World excluding Europe   All Rights Reserved.

unit 4

Most singing occurs on vowel sounds. There are some voiced consonants like z, m, and v, but it is the vowels which help us find an open throat and a secure sound. We make a vowel by changing the shape of the mouth and the position of the tongue. Read this phrase and notice how many different vowel sounds there are:

'There are many apples in an orchard.'

As singers we need to be clear about which vowel we are singing or the sound can lose intensity and accuracy. Here are some exercises for you to practise (you may like to do them in front of a mirror).

The five vowels: ah, eh, ee, oh and oo

You remember we looked at this in Unit 2. Place the tip of your tongue at the base of your lower teeth and say the vowels 'ah-eh-ee-oh-oo' without moving the tip of the tongue, but allowing the lips to round naturally. What happens to the tongue? Make sure it moves without the jaw. (If the jaw is moving a lot then gently place a finger lightly on the chin to immobilize it.) Try singing this exercise:

CD 1
24

This next exercise really gets your tongue working. Make sure the tip is touching the back of your bottom teeth. Try and keep your jaw still and allow your tongue to do the work as you move from the 'oo' to 'ee' shape. Keep an eye on your progress in a mirror!

CD 1
25

Now you have practised the vowel sounds, try singing this exercise with a confident 'v' before each vowel:

CD 1
26

Vowels with more than one sound

Vowels which are made up of two sounds are called **diphthongs** and occur when we glide from one vowel sound to another – as in the words 'take', 'now' and 'toy'. It's important the tongue works to make the change and not the jaw. Here are examples of the different English diphthongs:

'white'

'day'

'know'

'town'

'noise'

'new'

English also has a series of **triphthongs** where there are three sounds together, as in 'player' or 'fire'. When singing diphthongs and triphthongs stay on the first part of the sound for as long as possible and tuck in the extra sound(s) at the last minute. The only diphthong which does not obey this rule is 'iu' where the singer must get onto the second part of the sound quickly, as in 'music' or 'new'.

> Here are some fun sentences that use diphthongs. Try making up some of your own!
>
> The <u>bear</u> went into the bar and had a <u>beer</u>
>
> <u>How now brown cow</u>
>
> <u>Oh no I saw</u> a cat with a hat!

Practise singing these diphthongs and triphthongs, listening carefully to the CD to help you. Make sure the second sound is delayed until the end of the note – except for the last two words: 'new' and 'flew'.

CD 1

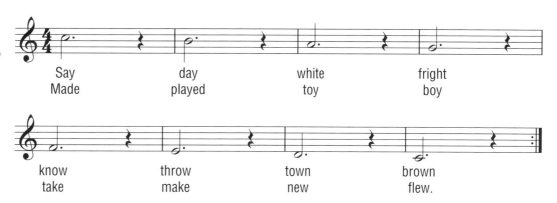

| Say | day | white | fright |
| Made | played | toy | boy |

| know | throw | town | brown |
| take | make | new | flew. |

> ### Did you know?
>
> English originated from the combination of languages and dialects brought to the east coast of Britain by the Germanic Anglo-Saxons in the 5th century. A great number of English words come from Latin roots, due partly to the influence of the Christian church. Modern English dates from around 1550 when the United Kingdom became a colonial power, early examples being the works of William Shakespeare and the King James Bible.

Check your posture

Stand with your back against a wall, feet a few inches away. Your head and the base of your spine should be in contact with the wall (you may need to adjust your pelvis slightly to achieve this). Shoulders should be down and knees not locked. Breathe in deeply and slowly, making sure you stay in contact with the wall.

An exercise to get the breath flowing

Breathe in through your nose, allowing the air to fill your lungs as deeply as possible. Let the air out on a vocalised 'ssss' sound to a slow and steady count of six. When you get to six, let go of any air that is left over, relaxing the abdominal muscles. Do the same again but this time let the air out on a vocalised 'zzzzz' sound for six counts. Next time use a vocalised 'vvvvv' sound, then lip trill ('brummm') or a vocalised, rolled 'r'.

Practising the song

Here are some exercises to practise before you sing the next song. Hold the vowel steadily through the whole phrase. Watch out for the diphthong on 'night' – sing mostly on the first sound of the vowel and tuck the second sound in at the end. Using the CD as a guide, sing each word twice, a step higher each time.

fact file
Longer slurs do the same job as extension lines.

Practise humming this before singing the words. Are your lips buzzing? Wet them slightly to help them buzz and tickle, and imagine the sound is far forward on your lips.

Did you know?

Folk songs are generally songs with no known composers which were passed on orally, enabling people to transmit their history across the generations. Performing the songs also reduced the boredom of manual labour, the rhythm helping during synchronized repetitive tasks, and setting the pace of activities such as planting, reaping, threshing and weaving.

All through the night

This famous welsh song was included in the *Last Night of the Proms* for many years.

Make the sound as smooth as possible by singing through and lengthening the vowels. Practise singing only on the vowel sounds first – this is quite tricky but a fun and useful exercise!

top tip Don't forget the diphthong in 'night'. Sing three counts on 'na' and at the last moment add the second sound 'eet'.

Welsh folksong

Gently ♩ = 96

mp

Long vowel here

Sleep my love, and peace at - tend thee, All through the night.
While the moon her watch is keep - ing, All through the night.

Guar - dian an - gels God will send thee, All through the night.
While the wea - ry world is sleep - ing, All through the night.

p

Soft the drow - sy hours are creep - ing, Hill and vale in slum - ber sleep - ing,
O'er thy spi - rit gent - ly steal - ing, Vi - sions of de - light re - veal - ing,

Can you manage the last line in one breath?

I, my lov - ing vi - gil keep - ing All through the night.
Breathes a pure and ho - ly feel - ing All through the night.

Did you find that last line tricky to sing in one breath? Try this exercise to extend your breath flow:

- Blow out air as though you're cooling a hot drink. Then relax your abdominal muscles and breathe in through your nose, as deeply as you can.

- Let the air out on a strong 'sss' to a count of 5, then let go of any air left over and relax your muscles.

- Do the same again but this time to a count of 10, then try counts of 15 and 20. See how far you can go!

Off-beat rhythms

The start of the verse of this song has a slightly tricky off-beat rhythm: 'looked over Jordan and...' The stress is on 'o' and 'Jor' so we need to bounce quickly onto those syllables. Try practising saying 'coffee and cream' first, and then the song words:

Cof - fee and cream, I like cof - fee and cream, I like cof - fee and cream, I like...
Looked o - ver Jor - dan, and looked o - ver Jor - dan, and looked o - ver Jor - dan, and...

CD 1
31

Swing low, sweet chariot

This well-known spiritual is often chanted by English rugby union fans at matches.

American spiritual

Soulfully ♩ = 80

Swing low, sweet cha - ri - ot,___ Com - ing for to car - ry me home; Swing_ low, sweet cha - ri - ot,___ Com - ing for to car - ry me home. I looked o - ver Jor - dan, and what did I see,___ Com - ing for to car - ry me home; A

Surprise!

band_ of an - gels com - ing af - ter me, Com - ing for to car - ry me home.

Swing low, sweet cha - ri - ot,___ Com - ing for to car - ry me home; Swing low, sweet cha - ri - ot,___ Com - ing for to car - ry me home.

unit 5

Consonants are formed mainly by the tongue and lips. The tongue flicks and hits the teeth or the roof of the mouth while the lips change shape. Consonants can be categorised as either **voiced** (which can be sung) or **unvoiced** (which are just air).

Voiced consonants: b, d, g, l, j, m, n, r, v, w, y, z

Unvoiced consonants: c, f, h, k, p, q, s, t, x

In English, consonants can change depending on how they are combined and what they precede.

Practise saying these consonants as you ask yourself:

- Where is my tongue?
- Do I use the tip, blade (middle) or back of the tongue to make the consonant?
- Can I say the consonant without involving my jaw?

Try saying the consonants again first loudly and then softly, observing the change in mood and intensity.

Sing this descending scale, allowing only your tongue to work. Watch yourself in a mirror.

top tip Remember, the jaw should have as little involvement as possible (it is primarily for chewing!). The tongue is a big muscle and can become lazy if the jaw is tense. Make sure the tongue is working independently from the jaw.

CD 1
32

```
Loo   loo   loo   loo   loo   loo   loo   loo____
Da    da    da    da    da    da    da    da____
Tea   tea   tea   tea   tea   tea   tea   tea____
Ga    ga    ga    ga    ga    ga    ga    ga____
Keh   keh   keh   keh   keh   keh   keh   keh____
```

Tongue twisters

Here are some fun tongue twisters to get your tongue and lips moving. Remember, the jaw shouldn't do much at all!

CD 1
33

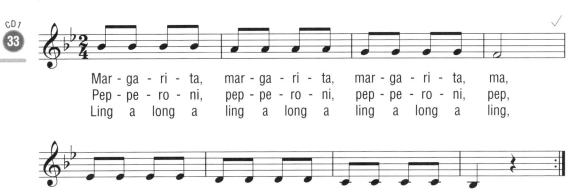

```
Mar - ga - ri - ta,   mar - ga - ri - ta,   mar - ga - ri - ta,   ma,
Pep - pe - ro - ni,   pep - pe - ro - ni,   pep - pe - ro - ni,   pep,
Ling  a  long  a      ling  a  long  a      ling  a  long  a      ling,

mar - ga - ri - ta,   mar - ga - ri - ta,   mar - ga - ri - ta,   ma.
pep - pe - ro - ni,   pep - pe - ro - ni,   pep - pe - ro - ni,   pep.
ling  a  long  a      ling  a  long  a      ling  a  long  a      ling.
```

23

The next song requires clear diction to give vitality and animation to the rhythm while conveying the simple sentiment. The most important factor here is energy and commitment to the words whilst keeping it flowing. Read the words aloud first and see if you can get your tongue to do most of the work. The music bounces along at quite a speed which means you need to breathe quickly too.

Simple gifts

This Shaker song was written by Joseph Brackett in 1848. The Shakers believed that everyone could find God within themselves rather than through the clergy or rituals. The Shakers wrote thousands of songs which were incorporated into their worship – this is one of the most famous after it was used by Aaron Copland in *Appalachian spring* and Sydney Carter used it as his inspiration for the hymn *Lord of the Dance*.

Joseph Brackett

Brightly ♩ = 116

'Tis the gift to be sim - ple, 'tis the

gift to be free, 'Tis the gift to come down where you ought to be, And

when we find our-selves in the place just right, 'Twill be in the val - ley of love and de-light.

When true sim - pli - ci - ty is gained, To bow and to bend we shan't be a-shamed, To

turn, turn will be our de-light, Till by turn - ing, turn - ing we come round right.

fact file

Accidentals are symbols which alter the pitch of a note by a semitone (the smallest step).
♯ = **sharp** = raises the pitch by a semitone
♭ = **flat** = lowers the pitch by a semitone
♮ = **natural** = cancels a sharp or flat.

Flash, bang, wallop! from 'Half a sixpence'

This song is great fun to sing. Some of the phrases are tongue twisters, so practise saying them first. The music moves along very quickly!

Reading the dots

$\frac{2}{2}$ = 2 x ♩ minims (**half notes**) per bar

Stems going up and down show there are different rhythms for different verses.

Words and Music by David Heneker

© 1963 Chappell Music Ltd   Reproduced by permission of Alfred Publishing Co Inc for World excluding Europe   All Rights Reserved.

unit 6

So far we have looked at five-note scales and tonic triads. Here's an example in F major:

Five note scale: | Tonic triad:

1 2 3 4 5 4 3 2 1 3 5 3 1

Can you sing these patterns yourself? You can start on any note which is comfortable.

In Unit 3 we looked at jumping up a fourth by singing the start of *Auld lang syne*. In this song you have a jump downwards. Follow the patterns in the music as you listen to the CD, and then try it by yourself.

CD 1
36

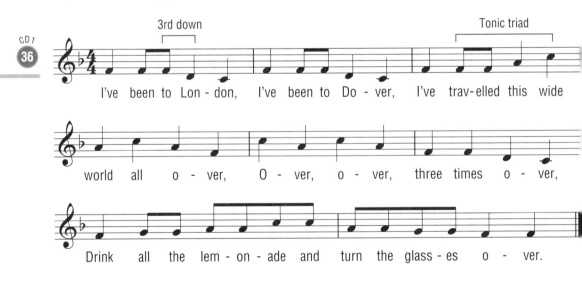

3rd down | Tonic triad

I've been to Lon - don, I've been to Do - ver, I've trav - elled this wide

world all o - ver, O - ver, o - ver, three times o - ver,

Drink all the lem - on - ade and turn the glass - es o - ver.

Practise these extracts by yourself first to make sure you can hear the **intervals**.

CD 1
37

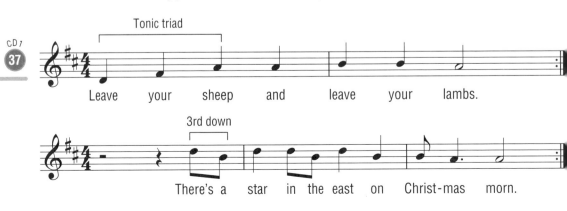

Tonic triad

Leave your sheep and leave your lambs.

3rd down

There's a star in the east on Christ - mas morn.

Rise up shepherd and foller

American folksong

In a funky style ♩ = 112

There's a star in the East on Christ-mas morn,
take good heed of the an-gels words,

Rise up shep-herd and fol-ler.

It will lead to the place where the
You'll for-get your flocks and for-

Sav-iour's born, Rise up shep-herd and fol-ler.
-get your herds,

Leave your sheep and leave your lambs, Rise up shep-herd and fol-ler.

Leave your ewes and leave your rams, Rise up shep-herd and fol-ler.

Fol-ler, fol-ler, Rise up shep-herd and fol-ler. Fol-ler the star of

Beth-le-hem, Rise up shep-herd and fol-ler. If you fol-ler.

quiz time

$\frac{4}{4}$ = _____

♩ ♩ ♩ ♩ are called _____

♩. is called a _____

♩ is called a _____

𝄽 is called a _____

New rhythm patterns and semiquavers

You will learn to recognise these groups and understand how the patterns sound.

Half-beat notes are called **quavers** (**eighth notes**) and are worth $^1/_2$ count; there are two of them to a beat:

A **semiquaver** (or **sixteenth note**) is worth $^1/_4$ count; there are four of them to a beat:

Here are some different semiquaver patterns which you often find in music.
Try clapping and saying them:

Man - ches - ter   U - ni - ted   Wol - ver - hamp - ton   Wan - der - ers

San Fran - cis - co   For - ty - ni - ners   Se - at - tle   Sea - hawks

We looked at dotted rhythms adding half as much again to a note's value on pages 12 and 15. The same is true of ♩. ♪ – the ♪ is worth $^3/_4$ of a beat, and the ♪ makes up the remaining $^1/_4$ of the count.

Generally rhythms are grouped by a beam to make up one full beat.

Try these exercises below, using the words to work out the rhythms. These patterns appear in the following song.

Ad - vent   ca - len - dar,   ad - vent   ca - len - dar,   ad - vent   ca - len - dar,   ad - vent   ca - len - dar.

In   the   dish - wash - er,   in   the   dish - wash - er,   in   the   dish - wash - er,   in   the   dish - wash - er.

Practising the song

This exercise practises jumping around the notes of the tonic triad. Can you make up your own patterns using these notes and words?

CD 1
39

I know who I   love,   I know who I   love,   I know, I know who I   love!

I know where I'm goin'

This folksong needs to be sung sensitively and wistfully. Watch out for the dynamics as they will really help tell the story.

Review

Dynamics are the letters given above the music which tell you how loud the music should be. They are abbreviations of Italian words. Here is the range you should know:

pp = *pianissimo* = very soft *mf* = *mezzo forte* = quite loud
p = *piano* = soft *f* = *forte* = loud
mp = *mezzo piano* = quite soft *ff* = *fortissimo* = very loudly

unit 7

Major and minor

So far the scales we have sung have been in **major** keys. In a **minor** key the third note of the scale is lower than in a major scale. This gives minor keys a sad sound. Using the CD, practise singing the start of some major and minor scales, making sure you can hear the difference:

Ma-jor ma-jor   ma-jor ma-jor   may   mi-nor mi-nor   mi-nor mi-nor   my

This exercise appears first in D major, then D minor:

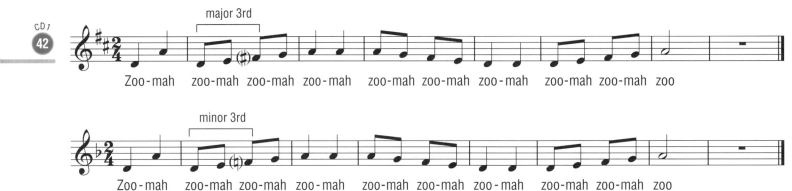

major 3rd

Zoo-mah   zoo-mah zoo-mah zoo-mah   zoo-mah zoo-mah zoo-mah   zoo-mah zoo-mah zoo

minor 3rd

Zoo-mah   zoo-mah zoo-mah zoo-mah   zoo-mah zoo-mah zoo-mah   zoo-mah zoo-mah zoo

A new time signature

The time signature **6/8** means there are six ♪ in each bar (measure). Each bar can be grouped into two main dotted crotchet (dotted quarter note) beats:

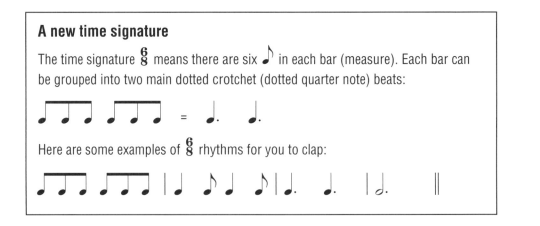

Here are some examples of **6/8** rhythms for you to clap:

Practising the song

Scarborough Fair has quite a few **diphthongs** (see p.19) at the end of phrases. Make sure the vowel is held purely and steadily for the whole phrase until the very end, when the diphthong should be inserted quickly and neatly.

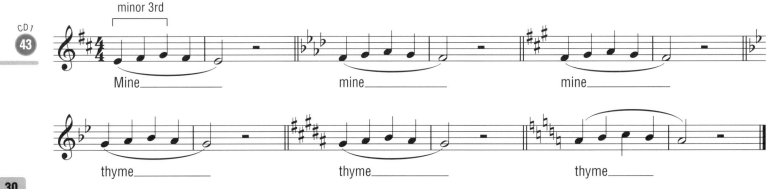

minor 3rd

Mine_____   mine_____   mine_____

thyme_____   thyme_____   thyme_____

Scarborough fair

In this song, a man asks the listener to pass on a message to his former lover in Scarborough.
She is to perform a series of impossible tasks in order for him to take her back. A great deal of
folklore was built around the herbs which are mentioned in this song. *Parsley* removes
bitterness in the stomach (and therefore in life); *sage* is a symbol of strength. *Rosemary*
represents love and faithfulness and *thyme* represents courage and strength.

English folksong

Sleep little baby

From now on, you should breathe where there are rests in the music. Breath marks (✓)
are only given when there is no rest. You may have noticed in this piece that the time
signature changes several times. Don't let it put you off – just keep counting silently.

fact file

Legato = smoothly
⌢ = pause

Peacefully ♩ = 74

Pam Wedgwood

p legato

mp

It's time to sleep, lit-tle ba-by, sleep.___ Lay down your

head lit-tle ba-by do not weep. May God pro - tect you and guide you on your

p

way, And may the sun shine up-on you ev-'ry day.

p

Hush now, hush now, close your lit-tle eyes When dark-ness

mp

falls and the nights are long,___ When stars are shi - ning bright-ly clear and

mp

strong, I'll al - ways keep you___ safe - ly by my side, Then dawn will

break and your eyes will o - pen wide. Hmm___ Hmm___

poco rit.
pp

Hmm___

Many people will not even attempt a note beyond their perceived range, but actually it's quite possible to extend how high or low you can sing.

- Begin by making a siren sound through your nose and then slide or glide up and down, from the lowest sound you can make to the highest. Keep a check on your head – make sure it doesn't go up and down with the sound!

- Now imagine you are sitting at the front of a rollercoaster and holding onto the bars in front of you. Push down on the bar and siren up, then lift the arms up and siren down. Follow the line below:

- Now try the same exercises on a lip trill (*brumm*) or rolled 'r'.

It's crucial not to carry too much weight on the sound as this can stop you from reaching higher notes. Try this exercise, making sure you keep the sound light and lively.

Now sing these **arpeggios** up and down, imagining the notes are going *down* rather than *up* and vice versa! Watch that your head stays level.

Without realising it, our body can become tense as we sing higher. Whilst singing these exercises, gently swing your arms by your side. As you approach the top of the arpeggio, the swing becomes more energetic, so that your arms fly up over your head in a big arch. Try bending your knees at the same time!

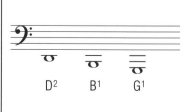

Did you know?

One of the lowest notes demanded in the classical repertoire is D2 (almost two octaves below middle C) in Osmin's second aria in Mozart's opera *Die Entführung aus dem Serail*. The lowest note for a choir is in Mahler's 8th Symphony (bar 1457 in the 'Chorus mysticus') and Rachmaninoff's *Vespers* requires B1. In Russian choirs the oktavists traditionally sing an octave below the bass, down to G1.

CD 1

Silent night

The organ in the Austrian church of St Nicholas was broken, so Gruber composed this simple melody with a guitar accompaniment. It was first sung on Christmas Eve in 1818 and has become one of the world's most famous and loved Christmas carols.

Don't forget to put a good 't' on the end of 'night' and watch out for the diphthongs.

Franz Xavier Gruber
Joseph Mohr

Gently ♪ = 116

p 1. Si - lent night, ho - ly night, All is calm,
mp 2. Si - lent night, ho - ly night, Shep-herds quake

all is bright, Round yon Vir - gin Mo - ther and Child, Ho - ly In - fant so
at the sight, Glo - ries stream_ from hea - ven a - far, Heav'n - ly hosts_ sing

ten - der and mild, Sleep in hea - ven - ly peace,_ Sleep_ in hea - ven - ly peace.
'Al - le - lu - ia', Christ, the Sa - viour is born,_ Christ, the Sa - viour is born.

mf

pp
Si - lent night, ho - ly night, Son of God, love's pure light,

Ra - diant beams from thy Ho - ly face, With the dawn of re - deem - ing grace,

poco rit.
pp
Je - sus, Lord, at thy birth,_ Je - sus, Lord, at thy birth.

> ### Did you know?
>
> In music, the words used to describe how music should be performed are usually in Italian. We have already looked at dynamics (see page 29). Tempo markings at the start of a piece can also be in Italian.
>
> **Poco rit** (**ritenuto**) means 'slow down a little' (**poco** means 'little').

Greensleeves

This traditional English song from the Tudor period is said to have been written by
Henry VIII for Anne Boleyn, although this has never been proved. There is a reference
to the 'Greensleeves' tune in Shakespeare's *The Merry Wives of Windsor*. 'Let the sky
rain potatoes! Let it thunder to the tune of Greensleeves!'

English folksong

A - las, my love,___ you
have been rea - dy

do me wrong___ To cast me off___ dis - cour - teous - ly: And I have lov - éd
at your hand___ To grant what - ev - er you would crave. I have both wa - gered

you so long,___ De - light - ing in___ your com - pa - ny. } Green - sleeves___ was
life and land,___ Your love___ and good___ will for to have. }

all my joy___ And Green - sleeves___ was my de - light. Green - sleeves___ my

heart of gold,___ And who but my la - dy Green - sleeves? Well I I will pray___ to

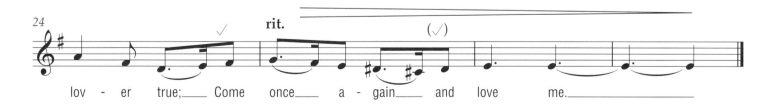

God on high___ That thou my con - stan - cy may see. For I am still___ thy

rit.

lov - er true;___ Come once___ a - gain___ and love me.___

unit 9

Trace your tongue over the roof of your mouth. At the front, and behind the top teeth, you will feel the **alveolar ridge**. A little further back and you will feel the domed **hard palate**. Now curl it towards the back of your mouth and the texture will feel squashy: this is the **soft palate**.

The **soft palate** is a soft muscular flap coming out of the hard palate and acts a little like a trap-door. Its primary use is to stop food and drink travelling up into our nose when we eat. We would also find it quite difficult to suck or blow without it.

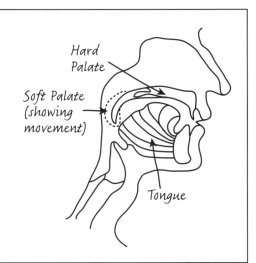

Hard Palate

Soft Palate (showing movement)

Tongue

An open throat

You may have heard people referring to an '**open throat**'. This is when the soft palate is high (as in the experiment above) but not too high so we end up sounding as though we have a blocked nose. Watch out that your tongue doesn't pull back and down in the process.

Try these exercises to experiment with an open throat.

Pretend you have a blocked nose and try to speak. The soft palate is lifted up against the back of the throat. Now speak with a nasal voice: the soft palate is much lower, resulting in too many vibrations going through the nose.

Imagine you have just been given a wonderful present and sigh, saying the word 'Ah'! You should feel the soft palate expand at the back of your throat. The same thing happens when you yawn or when we smell something lovely. It's a feeling of surprise!

Choose a comfortable note and hum it. Pinch your nose and notice that the sound stops. This time sing the word 'ah' with an open throat. Pinch your nose and the sound should continue without any change.

The singer has everything within him. The notes come out from his very life. They are not materials gathered from outside.
Rabindranath Tagore

The following exercises start with an 'ng', as in the word 'singing', and then open out to a clear sound – 'ah'. Check that your 'ah' is clear by pinching your nose!

top tip Make sure there is no break between 'ng' and 'gah'. Feel the lifting of the soft palate as you open to the 'ah' sound. Listen to the CD to help you.

CD *1*
50

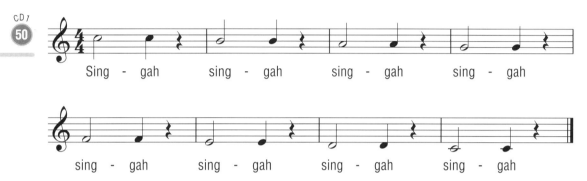

Thinking about the high notes

In this exercise, briefly pinch your nose at the * and then let go. The sound should be clear and should not have changed.

CD *1*
51

If you open your mouth too much at the front it can cut off the back of the throat and stop your soft palate from working effectively. Try making a small ring with your thumb and forefinger and hold it a few inches from your mouth. Sing into this circle and make sure your mouth doesn't open beyond the ring.

When starting on a high note, imagine that you have seen something surprising just before you sing. You should feel the back of the throat get slightly bigger as the soft palate moves. Try to keep this feeling of surprise as you sing down a five-note scale:

CD *1*
52

quiz time

Mezzo piano = _____

Descrescendo = _____

Poco rit = _____

♩ = 88 = _____

Practising the song

Before you sing the next song, prepare with these arpeggios and jumps:

fact file

A **scale** is made up of 8 notes. An **arpeggio** is very similar to a tonic triad, but has the 8th note added at the top – so is made up of notes 1, 3, 5 and 8 of any scale.

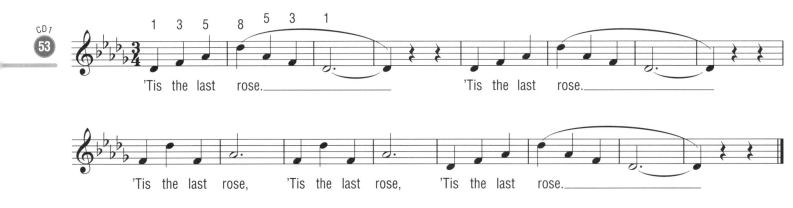

'Tis the last rose._____ 'Tis the last rose._____

'Tis the last rose, 'Tis the last rose, 'Tis the last rose._____

The last rose of summer

This poem has been an inspiration for many composers. The poet Thomas Moore
was a friend of Byron and Shelley. Make sure your tongue flicks for all the words
starting with 'l' – e.g. last, left, lovely. Keep working with the mirror!

Thomas Moore
John Stevenson

Expressively ♩ = 82

'Tis the last rose of___ sum-mer left___ bloom-ing___ a -
soon may I___ fol - low, when_ friend - ships de -

6

-lone; All her love - ly com - pan-ions are___ fa - ded___ and___ gone. No
- cay, And from love's shi - ning___ cir - cle the___ gems drop_ a - way! When_

11

flow'r of___ her___ kin - dred, No___ rose - bud___ is___ nigh_____ To re-
true hearts_ lie___ with - er'd, And___ fond ones___ are___ flown,_____ Oh!_

15

|1. | |2. |

-flect back her___ blush-es, or___ give sigh_ for___ sigh. So___ - lone?_____
who would in - ha - bit this___ bleak world a -

How can I keep from singing?

Versions of this song have been recorded by many vocal artists including Aled Jones,
Enya and Eva Cassidy.

Robert Lowry and
Ira David Sankey

Classify your voice

It can be useful to know what voice type you have, particularly if you are planning to sing in a choir. Voice classification is not only determined by range but also by colour, weight and where the voice feels most comfortable for the majority of the time.

Essentially there are seven vocal groupings:

- **soprano**, **mezzo-soprano**, **contralto** (female voices)
- **counter-tenor**, **tenor**, **baritone** and **bass** (male voices)

Within those voice types there are sub-divisions (such as 'lyric', 'dramatic', 'coloratura') but for now we will focus on the seven basic voice types. Here are their approximate ranges:

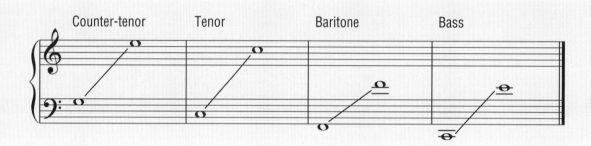

Singing in a choir

Choral music tends to divide voices into four categories – **soprano**, **alto**, **tenor** and **bass**. Since many people have medium-range voices, a choice has to be made which way to go in a choir. A mezzo-soprano or baritone will have to decide whether to go up (soprano/tenor) or down (alto/bass). A good singing teacher will help you work out what's best for you, but be prepared to change as your singing technique improves and your voice develops. You may start out an alto and end up a soprano, or vice versa.

Do remember though, it is always better not to sing at the extremes of the vocal range but work from the middle outwards. As the famous American singing teacher William Vennard said:

'I never feel any urgency about classifying a beginning student. So many premature diagnoses have been proved wrong, and it can be harmful to the student and embarrassing to the teacher to keep striving for an ill-chosen goal. It is best to begin in the middle part of the voice and work upward and downward until the voice classifies itself.'

Learning the notes of a song is just the start. Our ultimate goal is to communicate a mood or tell a story: the words are the key. Here are some points to bear in mind.

- Read through the poem or lyrics and make sure you completely understand them.
- Think about where you are going to breathe in order to interpret the words well.
- Use dynamics to colour the phrases, particularly if the words are quite repetitive. You rarely say the same thing twice in exactly the same way so think of different ways of performing each repetition.
- Don't over-enunciate the words but ensure they make sense to the listener so they can follow the meaning.
- Memorise the words so you can perform the song without the music. Your face and in particular your eyes are crucial in communicating the meaning and mood of a song.

Interpreting a song

Before you begin a song ask yourself these questions:

1 What is the song about?
2 Does the song have an overall mood?
3 Can you summarise the song in five words or less?
4 Does the song have a narrator or a character?
5 Where is your song set?
6 Are you singing to one person or many (or perhaps no-one at all)?
7 What has happened in the story before this song?
8 Are there moments of sadness or humour?

After singing the song, ask yourself these questions:

1 Does the character change from the beginning to the end of the song?
2 Does the song require a response or is it an ending?
3 What happens next in the story?

Here are two songs for you to try to interpret, with a little background information on each:

Skye boat song

This is a Scottish folksong about Bonnie Prince Charlie and his escape (aided by Flora MacDonald) from Uist to the Isle of Skye after his defeat at Culloden in 1746. His battle was against King George II's son, the Duke of Cumberland, and after he fled, he lived the rest of his life in exile.

Embraceable you

This song was originally written by George and Ira Gershwin for an unpublished operetta called 'East is West' but eventually included in the Broadway musical 'Girl Crazy' which became 'Crazy for You'. In this latter version, Polly Baker, a post mistress in Deadrock, falls in love with Bobby Child, a banker, (masquerading as 'Zangler'), an impresario who is putting on a show to save her father's ailing theatre. Polly has a brash exterior but underneath her bravado she longs for a man she can love.

Skye boat song

Scottish folksong

Flowing ♩. = 45

Speed bon-nie boat, like a bird on the wing, On - ward the sai - lors cry;

Car - ry the lad that's born to be king O - ver the sea to Skye.

f 1. Loud the winds howl, loud the waves roar, Thun - der - claps rend the air;
p 2. Though the waves leap, soft shall ye sleep; O - cean's a roy - al bed;

Baf - fled, our foes stand by the shore; Fol - low they will not dare.
Rocked in the deep, Flo - ra will keep watch by your wea - ry head.

Speed bon-nie boat, like a bird on the wing, On - ward the sai - lors cry;

FINE

Car - ry the lad that's born to be king O - ver the sea to Skye.

Big Breath!

mf 3. Ma - ny's the lad fought on that day Well the clay - more* could wield,
mf 4. Burned are our homes, ex - ile and death Scat - ter the loy - al men,

2nd time al Fine

mp When the night came si - lent - ly lay Dead on Cul - lo - den's field.
mp Yet ere the sword cool in the sheath *f* Char - lie will come a - gain.

Claymore = a two-handed Scottish sword

42

Embraceable you

*Music and Lyrics by George Gershwin
and Ira Gershwin*

© 1930 (renewed) Chappell & Co Inc and New World Music Co Ltd   Warner/Chappell North America Ltd
GERSHWIN® and GEORGE GERSHWIN® are registered trademarks of Gershwin Enterprises   IRA GERSHWIN™ is a trademark of Gershwin Enterprises
Reproduced by permission of Alfred Publishing Co Inc for World excluding Europe   All Rights Reserved.

Dynamics

Dynamics are the volume controls in music and a very useful tool in the aid to communication. Experiment with several different dynamic layers rather than just thinking of loud and soft. If you've been singing loudly for a while try singing softly – this will encourage your audience to really listen to what you are saying and draw them in.

Dynamics are given in Italian in music. See page 29 for a listing.

Messa di voce

If you have a long held note, try shaping the note with a *crescendo* and *diminuendo*. This technique is called **messa di voce** ('placing the voice'). Increase the breath pressure to increase the volume while holding the vowel pure and steady. Make sure the vowel stays the same as you *diminuendo* and see if you can finish at the same volume you started. Try this exercise to practise it:

Look at a fixed point on a wall and send the sound to that point. Keep the air flowing but gradually increase the amount to get louder then decrease the amount to get softer. It is much harder to *diminuendo*!

Shenandoah

The Shenandoah River is in the US states of Virginia and West Virginia and is surrounded by the Blue Ridge and the Appalachian Mountains. Look out for the dynamics in this song.

American folksong

The water is wide

The words are very important in this song – there is a change of mood at the end which you should try to colour with dynamics and vocal quality. Verse 2 has a lot of alliteration – extra weight could be given to those words beginning with 's'. Verse 3 has lots of crisp consonants – back, oak, broke, thinking … Can you roll your 'r' on broke for a fuller effect?

Traditional

Passionately ♩ = 66

1. The wa-ter is wide_____ I can-not get o'er. And nei-ther have I_____ the wings to__ fly. Give me a boat_____ that can car - ry__ two, And both shall row,_____ my true love and I.

2. A ship there is_____ and she sails the seas. She's la - den deep,_____ as deep can_ be; But not so deep_____ as the love I'm_ in, And I know not if_____ I sink or swim.

3. I leaned my back_____ a - gainst a young oak, Think - ing that he_____ were a trust - y__ tree; But first he bend - ed and then he__ broke; Thus did my love_____ prove false to me.

4. O love is hand - some and love is fine, Bright as a jewel_____ when first it's__ new; But love grows old_____ and wax - es__ cold And fades a - way like the morn - ing dew.

unit 11

As singers we are interested in the larynx as an instrument for making sound, but its main function is to stop food going down the windpipe! When we swallow, the top of the larynx acts like a valve and closes over the windpipe so the food goes down the oesophagus into the stomach. When we sing, we need that valve to be free and open – that's why it's never a good idea to eat and sing at the same time!

The **larynx** is made up of cartilage and bone which fit together like a three-dimensional moveable puzzle. The **vocal folds** (or cords as they used to be known) are held inside and the length and thickness by which they vibrate determines the pitch produced. The longer and thinner they are, the higher the pitch.

How we sing

When you breathe in, the space between the vocal folds opens up to allow the air in. As the air comes back up the windpipe the folds come together and vibrate. How they come together effects the quality of the sound. If the air pressure is too forceful this can result in a hard attack to the note; if the air pressure is too fast the fold might not come together properly – resulting in a breathy sound.

Improving your quality of sound

Here are some exercises to practise. Hear the first note clearly in your head before you sing it – don't slide up to the notes! Aim for a free and easy open throat, with no explosive starts to the sound.

CD2
6

Sing very definitely through the z and v:

CD2
7

top tip Aim for a wide open throat and free larynx that can move and vibrate without restraint when singing. Be careful not to force the larynx into any particular position.

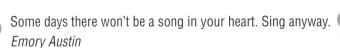

Some days there won't be a song in your heart. Sing anyway.
Emory Austin

Resonance

Singing is unique and personal – no two voices are alike. There are many different areas which act as **resonators** and influence our vocal quality: the larynx, the mouth and sometimes even the nose. We can move and change the shape of some of these areas which also affects the sound that we produce.

Experimenting with the sound quality

You may have heard singers say they feel a certain sound in their eyes, nose or at the top of their head. These are all perceptions which help singers manipulate their vocal quality. Of course some of them are physically impossible, but many singers are convinced that thinking about them does alter the sound. A teacher will be able to help you distinguish fact from fiction and help you develop your full potential.

Exploring resonance

- Make a humming sound with your mouth shut and teeth clenched. You should feel the vibration mainly in your nose.
- Try it again with your teeth as far apart as possible without opening your mouth. This time the vibrations should feel deep in your throat.
- Have another go but with your teeth slightly apart. Your lips may start to tingle!
- Choose a comfortable note to hum. When you feel your lips starting to tickle, open you mouth and change into a vowel sound (moooo, meeeee, maaaa).

Now sing through the 'mm' (aim for tickly lips!) and open onto the vowel:

Close immediately onto the 'ng', then open into a clear 'a', feeling the action in the soft palate.

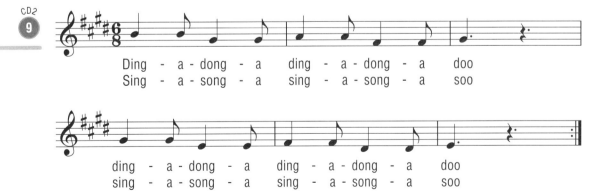

Be really percussive here the with 'ng' sound.

47

Let's face the music and dance

This song is great fun. There are plenty of words beginning with 'm' – moonlight,
music, moon - as well as others with emphasised 'm' syllables – romance, humming.
Sing through the 'm' before opening onto the vowel.

fact file
Moderato = at a moderate pace

Words and Music by Irving Berlin

© 1936 Irving Berlin Music Corp   Warner/Chappell Music Ltd
Reproduced by permission of Alfred Publishing Co Inc for World excluding Europe   All Rights Reserved.

Hushabye Mountain   from 'Chitty chitty bang bang'

This lovely lullaby benefits from long, sustained breaths. Try singing
the song on the vowels only first to ensure a smooth vocal line.

Words and Music by
Richard M. Sherman and Robert B. Sherman

© 1968 EMI Unart Catalog, Inc   All Rights Controlled by EMI Unart Catalog, Inc (Publishing) and Alfred Music Publishing Co., Inc (Print)
All Rights Reserved. Used by permission

Remember when

This beautiful nostalgic song was written especially for the book.

Pam Wedgwood

unit 12

Many people get worried when they approach high notes and this creates tension. Help is at hand! First of all, let's not call it a high note (psychologically this is not good or helpful) – instead we'll call it the rogue note! The next few songs have been chosen especially because they have large leaps up to notes which could be thought of as high. Here are some strategies for mastering high notes.

Preparation

Make sure your posture is well balanced so that you can breathe correctly. Check that your jaw is not shooting up or forwards and remember the feeling of surprise which creates plenty of space inside the mouth. Don't over-open the front of the mouth and keep your jaw relaxed and free. Next use some of your warm-up techniques and siren ('ng') throughout your vocal range, blow some raspberries or lip trills (see page 33 for details).

Vowels on rogue notes

Some vowels are easier to sing than others. A closed vowel like 'ee' can be quite tricky. Experiment with singing a vowel that is comfortable on the rogue note. Now keep that shape but sing the other 'rogue' vowel in your head. You might be surprised to hear the right sound!

Consonants on rogue notes

It could be that a consonant on the rogue note is giving you difficulty. Try singing the phrase on the vowels only – leaving out all the consonants. When you can do this successfully include the consonants again, but very lightly.

Brain teasers

If you are still finding it awkward try some of the following ideas. Start by singing the phrase in a range that is comfortable. Gradually move the music up by step whilst attempting these exercises:

- Imagine you are holding the note in your hands and you are about to put it on a shelf high above your head. Lift the note over the shelf and place it down on the shelf – as the note hits the shelf you sing your rogue note.
- Imagine you are on a rollercoaster which is climbing to the top of its run. As you tip over the top, sing your rogue note and bend your knees at the same time!
- Gently swing your arms by your side. As you approach the rogue note, the arms become more energetic, so they fly up over your head. Try bending your knees at the same time.

---

top tip Our bodies can become tense as we approach something we're worried about: the rogue note. We need to trick our body into relaxing so that a rogue note is more achievable.

Warming up

Before singing the next song, let's warm up your body and voice.

- Lower your head towards your chest, feeling a stretch at the back of your neck. Breathe in slowly and lift your head to its natural position and blow out all the air. Do this three times.

- Imagine you are sitting at the front of a rollercoaster and holding onto the bar in front of you. Push down on the bar and siren up, then lift your arms up and siren down. Follow your own rollercoaster path. We first tried this in unit 8 – see p.33 for more details.

As you sing this exercise, think 'up' as you come down, in order to stop the pitch from going flat:

fact file

An **octave** is an interval of 8 notes – the top and bottom notes always have the same note name.

Here, think down to the top note. Bend your knees just before the top note.

top tip The 'g' in 'signora' makes a 'nyo' sound – 'sinyora'.

Practising the song

Imagine the top note ('heart') is at the same pitch as the other notes. Check your head doesn't shoot up when you reach it – lots of surprise and a raised soft palate on 'heart' will help. Slightly change the vowel shape on 'keep' so it is more like 'heart'.

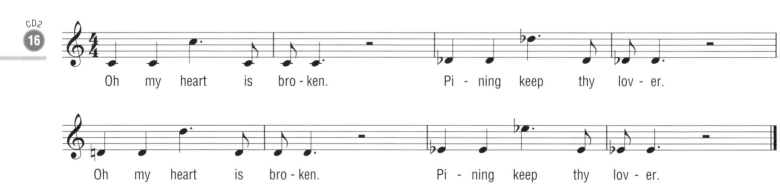

Practise singing this line on 'Yoh' first, then with the vowels only. Keep the vowels open on the top notes (lots of surprise) and imagine the top notes are low! Trick your brain and check your head doesn't go up when singing higher. Make sure the vowel is not too tight and squeezed on the 'ee' of 'keep'.

Watching the wheat

This is one of Wales' best-known folksongs. It is a love song and has been linked
to the rich heiress Ann Thomas (1704-27) – the so-called 'Maid of Cefn Ydfa' –
who was being forced to marry against her will. She allegedly died of heartbreak
for her true love, the poet Will Hopcyn.

Welsh folksong

Thoughtfully ♩ = 84

(verse 1)
A simple youthful lad am I, Who loves at fancy's pleasure: I fondly watch the blooming wheat, Another reaps the treasure. Wherefore still despise my suit? Why pining keep thy lover? For some new charm thou matchless fair, I day by day discover.

(verse 2)
Each day reveals some new-born grace, Or does fond faith deceive me? In love to Him who formed thy face, With pity now receive me. Lift thine eyes, one look bestow. Give me thy hand, my fairest, For in thy bosom, lovely maid, My heart's true key thou bearest.

(verse 3)
While hair adorns this aching brow Still I will love sincerely, While ocean rolls its briny flow Still I will love thee dearly. Then tell the truth, in secret tell, And under seal discover, If it be I or who is blest As thy true heart's best lover.

Challenge

In this song we haven't given you any breath marks. You can take a breath wherever there is a rest – but you will need to breath in between these places as well. See if you can work out the best place to breathe each time and mark in your own ticks to remind you.

The next two songs have quite large vocal ranges so let's prepare with these exercises. Make sure the top note feels free – with lots of space inside the mouth. Consonants should be crisp and energetic. Try bending your knees just before the top note – or swinging your arms over your head!

More octave jumps

Sing these two exercises a step higher each time to prepare for the octave jumps in the next songs. Imagine the top note ('rose') is at the same pitch as the other notes and check your head doesn't shoot up for it. Lots of surprise (a raised soft palate) is needed, so anticipate that feeling on the lower notes in preparation for the rogue note. Don't drop heavily back down again – keep the lower notes light.

The 'm' of 'some' could be troublesome here – don't make too much of it and only allow your lips to touch very lightly. Allow your tongue to make the correct vowel sound for 'where', but aim for an oval mouth shape (check in a mirror!).

A **scotch snap rhythm** is ♪♩. It appears in Scottish dance music and you'll find it in *My love is like a red, red rose*. Practise speaking the example below to get the feel of the different dotted rhythms:

My love is like a red, red rose

The speaker of this poem is besotted with his lady and compares her to a red, red rose and a sweetly-played melody. He tells his beloved that although he must leave he will return for her, even if he has to travel ten thousand miles. It is the ultimate love song!

top tip Don't drop too heavily down to the bottom notes, or it will be too hard to climb up again.

Scottish folksong

Over the rainbow   from 'The Wizard of Oz'

Music by Harold Arlen
Lyrics by E. Y. Harburg

© 1938 Metro-Goldwyn-Mayer Inc   © 1939 EMI Feist Catalog Inc   All Rights Controlled and Administered by EMI Feist Catalog Inc (Publishing) and Alfred Music Publishing Co., Inc (Print)   All Rights Reserved. Used by Permission.

How to read vocal music

Solo vocal music is usually written with the voice part in the treble clef, irrespective of voice type (female or male). It is assumed that the male voice sings an octave lower.

Choral music can be printed in two ways – short score and open score.

Short score is often used for hymn books but you will come across it in choral works and oratorios. The soprano's notes are at the top with the stems pointing up. If the soprano part drops below the alto part the direction of the stems tell you which note to sing. The tenor reads his notes in the bass clef, stems up.

In **open score** each voice has its own vocal line. This is particularly useful if each part has a complicated or tricky rhythm, if the parts divide, or if the vocal lines cross each other many times. The tenor reads his notes in the treble clef but they sound an octave lower.

unit 13

Breath support and control are the power behind singing. This power comes from our abdominal muscles and breath control is achieved by training these muscles.

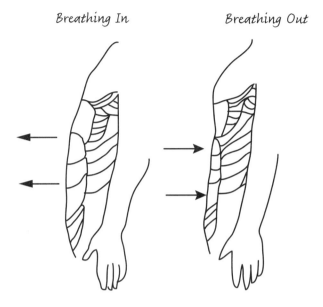

Breathing In   Breathing Out

We need to control the exhalation of air by using our abdominal muscles to prevent all the air escaping at once. Training these muscles takes time, but here are some exercises to help you become aware of them.

Imagine you have blown up a balloon and are holding the neck tightly to stop the air escaping. If you let go, the balloon will deflate quickly and fly around the room. Instead, support the bottom of the balloon with your other hand whilst allowing a little air to escape from the neck. The air seeps out and the shape of the balloon stays intact.

Kneel down on your hands and knees so you are on all fours. Blow out a stream of air, contracting your abdominal muscles in the process. Wait for a few seconds and then relax your abdominal muscles so they drop towards the floor. As you do this, open your mouth and let the air in.

Standing up, place one hand on your abdominal area. Hold the other hand about a shoulder width in front of your face and imagine you are trying to blow a feather off it. Give four short blows followed by one long blow. Your abdominal muscles should bounce in and out with each blow.

top tip Don't forget, when you breathe in your body expands. When you breathe out, everything contracts. In order for something to expand easily it shouldn't be tense or tight.

 The only thing better than singing is more singing.
Ella Fitzgerald

If you have ever had dance lessons you will remember the need to pull in the abdominal muscles. This is not so helpful for singing! Try pulling in your abdominal muscles and breathe in at the same time. It's quite difficult, isn't it? In order to breathe well and deeply, the singer must relax the abdominal muscles to allow the **diaphragm** to move. At the same time, the rib cage needs to be able to swing (which is why it is best to stand when singing), the shoulders should remain low and the breath should be as inaudible as possible.

> Take a deep breath in, then blow out the air as though you are cooling a hot drink. Relax the abdominal muscles and breathe in again through your nose, allowing the air to fill as deeply as possible. Let the air out on a strong 'sss' sound while counting in your head to 10. Relax the abdominal muscles and let go of any air that is left over. Breathe in again as before through the nose. Let the air out on a strong 'sss' sound for 15 seconds this time. Keep repeating this exercise for 16, 17, 18, 19 and 20 seconds. See how far you can go!

You may have felt a slight squeezing or tightening of the abdominal muscles when you did this exercise. This is not a vigorous sensation but a light pressure. When we are approaching high notes, we may wish to increase that pressure a little to help support the notes.

top tip If you suffer from a dry throat, try breathing through your nose rather than your mouth, as this can warm the air. A quick breath will have to come in through your mouth but sometimes there is time for a breath through the nose instead, particularly at the start of a song.

Revision

Try to remember the things we have looked at so far as you sing the next songs:
- Think down for high notes.
- Keep an oval mouth shape on high notes.
- Keep a relaxed, free and easy jaw.
- Use the tongue for certain consonants ('l', 't' and 'n').
- Lift the soft palate – by a feeling of 'surprise' – for the high notes.
- Relax the abdominal muscles before you take a breath.
- Look out for diphthongs.
- Keep an eye on your posture and your head and neck area.

Let's get singing!

Think down as you go up in both of these exercises. Bend your knees on the top note and feel free and flexible, making sure the jaw is relaxed.

Ya_____
Your_____

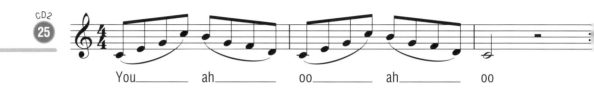

You_____ ah_____ oo_____ ah_____ oo

Sing the next phrases in one breath. Keep the consonants on the top notes clear and sing right through the vowel. Check your jaw feels free and your tongue is not pulled back down your throat. Aim for that surprised feel (raised soft palate) at the back of the throat and don't reach for the top note – think 'down' and trick your brain!

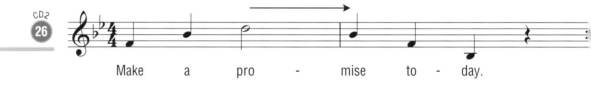

Make a pro - mise to - day.

Home is o - ver there.

I'll be here for you.

Oh what a morn - - ing!

Deep river

This African, American spiritual as been sung in several films including the
1929 film version of *Show Boat*. It is also sung as the closing spiritual in
Michael Tippett's oratorio *A Child of our Time*.

top tip Sing clearly through the first vowel
and feel lots of surprise for the top notes! Think
down, particularly for the top F in bar 15.

American spiritual

Did you know?

Spirituals are religious songs which as well as communicating a Christian meaning
also put across the hardships that were part of being an African-American slave. The
meaning of these songs was often covert. For example, a 'home' is a safe place
where everyone can live freely – so it can mean heaven or a free country.

Danny boy   Londonderry air

These words were written by English lawyer and lyricist, Frederic Weatherly in 1910
and fitted to the tune *Londonderry Air* in 1913. It has been recorded by countless
vocalists over the years from Elvis Presley to operatic soprano Elisabeth Schwarzkopf.

Irish folksong

The Lord is my shepherd   Words from Psalm 23

Howard Goodall is well known for his TV music – *Mr Bean*, *Blackadder*, *Red Dwarf* and *QI* – and he wrote this arrangement of Psalm 23 for *The Vicar of Dibley*.

fact file

These signs indicate multiple bars' rest put together. Each time here you need to count 2 bars.

Words From Psalm 23
Music by Howard Goodall

© 1994 Rights Worldwide Ltd   All Rights Reserved.

Unit 14

Let's begin developing your vocal agility by practising singing two or more notes to a syllable. It's important no aspirate (breathy) 'h' sounds creep in between the notes – keep the sound as smooth as possible.

Oo__ ee__ ay__ ah oo__ ee__ ah   oo__ ee__ ay__ ah oo__ ee__ ah

Try this exercise – the sound should be light and flowing. Your mouth will open slightly as you get higher.

Yoh_____   yoh_____

Yoh_____   yoh_____

This time you'll need a big breath – see if you can keep going through to the end. Then relax the abdominal muscles, let the air in and try again.

Yoh_____

Practise these phrases from *Down by the Salley Gardens* and *David of the white rock* to make sure they are really smooth: no bumps or aspirate 'h' sounds …

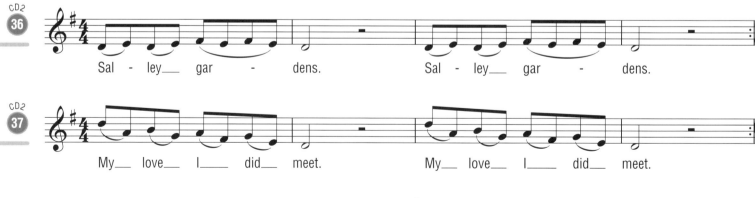

Sal - ley__ gar - dens.   Sal - ley__ gar - dens.

My__ love__ I__ did__ meet.   My__ love__ I__ did__ meet.

Wi - dow__ and__ chil - dren.__   Wi - dow__ and__ chil - dren.__

Down by the Salley Gardens

'Salley' or 'sally' is a form of the Standard English word 'sallow' and is close in sound to the Irish word 'saileach', meaning willow. According to Celtic lore, the willow is associated with enchantment and dreaming and should be planted in honour of a birth or marriage. Many composers have been inspired by this beautiful melody, such as Ivor Gurney and Benjamin Britten.

Words by William Butler Yeats
Irish folksong

Lyrics (verse 1 / verse 2):

Down by the Sal - ley Gar - dens my love and I did meet; She passed the Sal - ley Gar - dens with lit - tle snow - white feet. She bid me take life ea - sy, as the leaves grow on the tree; But I, be - ing young and fool - ish, with her would not a - gree. In a ...

field by the ri - ver my love and I did stand, And on my lean - ing shoul - der she laid her snow - white hand. She bid me take life ea - sy, as the grass grows on the weirs; But I was young and fool - ish, and now am full of ... tears.

Relaxed, free and easy jaw here

poco rit. (*2nd time*)

1. 2.

Did you know?

Opera brings together acting, scenery, costumes, music and singing in a large-scale performance. It will include soloists, a chorus and orchestra.

An **oratorio** is like an opera without scenery, props or costumes. The performance is static, without much interaction between the soloists, and the plots tend to be sacred.

A **cantata** is a musical work for choir with instrumental accompaniment, often in several movements. It is usually on a smaller scale than an oratorio and can be secular or sacred.

David of the White Rock

David Owen was a blind harpist and composer who lived near Porthmadog in Caernarfenshire, Wales in the first half of the 18th century. He was known as David of the White Rock because he lived at a farm called The White Rock. Tradition has it that as he lay dying at the age of 29, he called for his harp and composed this beautiful melody.

Welsh folksong

Bring__ me,__ said__ Da - vid, my harp__ I__ a - dore,__
Last__ night__ the__ voice of an an - gel__ did__ say,__

Be - fore death calls me,__ I'd play it__ once__ more,
'Come home - ward Da - vid,__ now I hear__ you__ play,'

Help me__ to__ reach the__ be - lov - ed strings a - gain,__ On
Fare - well__ my__ harp, Oh__ fare - well__ to__ your__ strings,__ I

wi - dow__ and__ chil - dren__ God's bless - ings re - main.
wish__ all__ my__ loved__ ones__ the bless - ing God brings.

Did you know?

A **libretto** is the text (or lyrics) of a musical work, which includes all the stage directions. Occasionally a composer might write his own but in most cases lyrics are written by someone else.

A cappella refers to unaccompanied choral singing. It originated in churches and actually means 'in the manner of the church' but now it can cover barbershop and close harmony singing.

SATB is the abbreviation for voices in a standard choir: soprano, alto, tenor, bass.

Vocal health

As your body is your instrument, it is important to look after it, not only so it functions well but also so that germs and illnesses are kept at bay. Bear in mind the following suggestions:

- Drink plenty of water as this can flush out germs and will keep your voice lubricated well. Water is particularly crucial on a long plane journey or in the car, as air conditioning can dry out the throat.

- Avoid too much tea, coffee and alcohol as they can also dehydrate the voice.

- Avoid shouting or speaking loudly particularly over background noise like in a pub or on long car journey.

- Get a good amount of sleep so your body and voice can function well.

- Avoid eating spicy foods late at night as this can cause acid reflux which can result in a sore throat.

- Wash your hands when you come into contact with someone who has a cold or illness – this will stop the germs spreading to you.

- Keep an eye on your posture. Make sure you can breathe well as this will put less strain on your voice.

What to do if you get a cold

- Drink plenty of water.
- Steam – put your head over a bowl of boiling water and cover your head with a towel. Breathe deeply inhaling the steam. Repeat this several times a day.
- Gargle with warm salt water but never with aspirin as this can damage the vocal folds.
- Avoid coughing and clearing your voice as this will not help.

It is possible to sing with a cold but not so good to sing with a sore throat. Never sing with laryngitis – it is like running on a sprained ankle – it will make it worse and could damage it. Completely rest the voice and inhale steam as this can be very effective in the healing process. Do not whisper as this is very tiring on the vocal folds.

Singing can have a direct impact on our physical and mental health. Some doctors believe that singing is a valuable aerobic exercise which encourages better posture and deeper breathing. It's thought that singing releases endorphins in the body, which can relieve pain and reduce stress. Using singing as a therapy for relaxation, overcoming depression and anxiety, and even treating clinically serious mental-health problems, is a growing movement.

unit 15

Notice your breathing right now. Your body is using just the right amount of air to function well. Our singing isn't helped if we take in too much air or if we force too much air out. Sometimes we need a quick breath, known as a **snatch breath**, as in *Ding dong merrily on high*. It should still be as deep as possible so we need to make sure the abdominal movement is the same – as the muscles become more flexible they will learn to respond quickly. Never breathe in the middle of a word unless it is one that goes on for an exceptionally long time (like 'Gloria') and make the breath as inaudible as possible.

Trying a snatch breath

Count aloud saying the following at a steady pace:

1 and 2 and 3 and 4 and 1 and 2 and 3 and 4 (snatch breath)

1 and 2 and 3 and 4 and 1 and 2 and 3 and 4 (snatch breath)

1 and 2 and 3 and 4 and 1 and 2 and 3 and 4 (snatch breath)

Make sure the snatch breath is quick so that number 1 is on time. Monitor your abdominal muscles by placing a hand on that area. Think about letting go of the muscles (relaxing) rather than breathing in. This will allow the air to flow in naturally.

If you find a snatch breath difficult, slow the song down and give yourself time for the breath. Then gradually speed up the tempo, always checking that the abdominal release is working.

top tip Check your posture does not collapse as you exhale the air. The rib cage needs to stay open otherwise the abdominal muscles below can become cramped and ineffective.

Practising the song

Sing this exercise slowly and take a snatch breath when you need to.

Ding - a - dong - a ding - a - dong - a ding - a - dong - a ding - a - dong - a

ding - a - dong - a ding - a - dong - a ding - a - dong - a ding - a - dong - a

ding - a - dong - a ding - a - dong - a ding - a - dong - a ding - a - dong - a ding.

The following songs need quick snatched breaths. See how you get on!

Ding dong merrily on high

Try singing 'Gloria' in one breath. If you find this tricky, take a breath
at one of the emergency breath marks.

Words by George Ratcliffe Woodward
Music by Thoinot Arbeau

Merrily ♩ = 132

f bell-like

sim.

Ding dong, mer - ri - ly on high, In heav'n the bells are ring - ing.
E'en so, here be - low, be - low, Let stee - ple bells be swung - en;

Ding dong, ve - ri - ly the sky, Is riv'n with an - gels sing - ing:
And i - o, i - o, i - o, By priest and peo - ple sung - en!

Glo - - - - - - - - - - -

- - - - - ri - a, Ho - san - na in ex - cel - sis.

Glo - - - - - - - - - - -

- - - - - ri - a, Ho - san - na in ex - cel - sis.

There's no business like show business

Words and Music by Irving Berlin

© 1946 Irving Berlin Music Corp   Warner/Chappell Music Ltd
Reproduced by permission of Alfred Publishing Co Inc for World excluding Europe   All Rights Reserved.

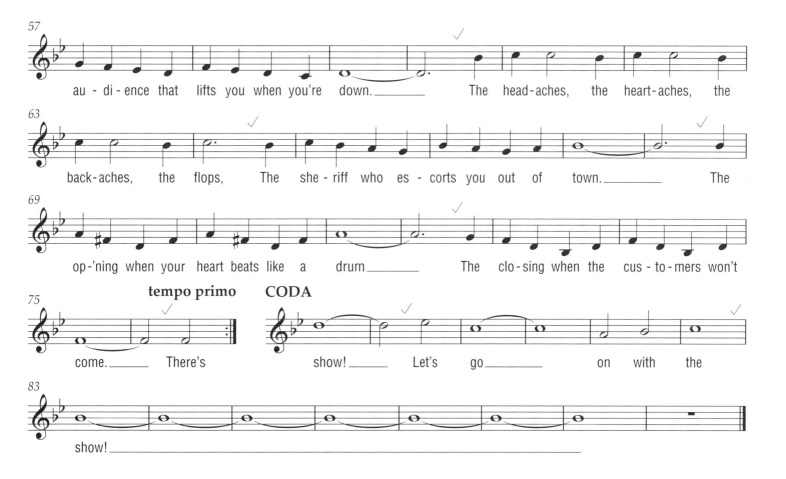

au - di - ence that lifts you when you're down._____ The head-aches, the heart-aches, the back-aches, the flops, The she - riff who es - corts you out of town._____ The op-'ning when your heart beats like a drum_____ The clo-sing when the cus - to-mers won't come._____ There's

tempo primo **CODA**

show!_____ Let's go_____ on with the

show!_____

Performing and nerves

Most people suffer from nerves when performing to a greater or lesser extent. Nerves can actually help a performance as they give a positive energy which can be turned into excitement. The issue comes if nerves are overwhelming. Obvious symptoms can be a dry throat or excessive sweating or shaking.

Here are some tips to help you overcome those nerves and give a good performance:

• The more you have practised the less nervous you are likely to be. If you are going to sing a song from memory, make sure it is memorised well in advance.

• Always arrive at the venue in plenty of time so that you are relaxed and calm before you perform.

• Make sure you have done a gentle warm-up including some posture and breathing exercises. Just before you go on stage, take some deep breaths and blow out the air slowly to calm your heart rate.

• Wear comfortable clothing and shoes so you are not distracted by an outfit that is too tight and stops you from breathing well or a pair of shoes that are too precarious and upset your posture and balance.

• Avoid dairy foods which can build up mucus in the throat and sugary products which can give you a rush and make you more jumpy.

• Don't focus on the difficult passage or note in a song. Rather think about the music as a whole and aim to communicate that feeling or emotion to the audience.

• At home, practise walking 'on stage', acknowledging your audience (bowing) and accompanist. Think about what you are going to do with your hands – you may be holding a microphone but if not, hang them loosely by your sides.

• Don't dwell on any negative moments in the performance – the audience is on your side and wants you to do well. They are usually less critical than you think and haven't come to watch you give yourself a critique as you perform.

• Believe in yourself and enjoy it! Performing can be an exhilarating and fun experience if you are prepared to let yourself go a little.

Concert pieces

Silent worship

In 1928 Arthur Somervell adapted the words of Handel's aria *Non lo dirò col labbro* and created 'Silent worship'. It has been a popular recital piece ever since and appeared in the film adaptation of Austen's *Emma*.

top tip Try to sing this as smoothly as possible.

Arthur Somervell
George Frederick Handel

Cry me a river

This jazzy blues ballad was originally written for Ella Fitzgerald. It starts on a high note so you need lots of 'surprise': remember to think down rather than up to this note. The middle section can be quite punchy and dramatic. Enjoy the text here and incorporate lots of expression and articulation.

Words and Music by Arthur Hamilton

© 1953 (renewed) Chappell & Co Inc and Harmony Grace Publishing   Warner/Chappell North America Ltd
Reproduced by permission of Alfred Publishing Co Inc for World excluding Europe   All Rights Reserved.

I can see clearly now

This song was a big hit for Johnny Nash in 1972 and has been covered by many artists over the years. The middle section has several long notes on the word 'sky'. It is possible to break this section with some breaths so some suggestions have been made for you.

© 1972 CP Masters BV and Nashco Music Inc   Warner/Chappell Music Publishing Ltd
Reproduced by permission of Alfred Publishing Co Inc for World excluding Europe   All Rights Reserved.

Singin' in the rain

In this famous dance routine from hit American film *Singin' in the Rain*, Kelly danced in water with a little bit of milk added so that the puddles and raindrops would show up better on film! The song has an octave jump at the start – just like *Over the rainbow*.

top tip Remember to think 'down' for the top note, keep a relaxed jaw and an eye on your posture (particularly the head and neck).

Music by Nacio Herb Brown
Lyrics by Arthur Freed

© 1929 Metro-Goldwyn-Mayer Corp   All Rights Controlled by EMI Robbins Catalog Inc (Publishing) and Alfred Music Publishing Co (Print)
All Rights Reserved   Used by permission.

Let's call the whole thing off

This song was written by George and Ira Gershwin for the 1937 film *Shall we dance?*

top tip You can have great fu
with the regional accents here.

Music and Lyrics by George Gershwin and Ira Gershw

© 1936 (Renewed) Chappell & Co Inc   Warner/Chappell North America Ltd
GERSHWIN® and GEORGE GERSHWIN® are registered trademarks of Gershwin Enterprises   IRA GERSHWIN™ is a trademark of Gershwin Enterprises
Reproduced by permission of Alfred Publishing Co Inc for World excluding Europe   All Rights Reserved.

Dear Lord and father of mankind

This popular hymn has been recorded by many choirs, soloists and
even pipe bands. The music gradually builds up in the middle of each
verse, but overall the feeling should be one of calm and stillness.

C.H.H. Parry

Dear Lord and fa - ther _ of man - kind, For -
sim - ple trust _ like _ theirs who heard, Be -

- give our fool - ish ways; Re - clothe us in our right - ful mind; In
- side the Sy - rian sea, The gra - cious call - ing of the Lord, Let

pu - rer lives thy ser - vice _ find In _ deep - er rev - 'rence _ praise, In
us, like them, with - out a _ word Rise _ up and fol - low _ thee, Rise

deep - er rev - 'rence praise. In Sab - bath rest _ by _ Ga - li - lee! O
up and fol - low thee. O thy still dews _ of _ qui - et - ness, Till

calm of hills a - bove, Where Je - sus knelt to share with thee The
all our stri - vings cease; Take from our souls the strain and stress And

si - lence of e - ter - ni - ty, In - ter - pre - ted _ by _ love! In -
let our or - dered lives con - fess The _ beau - ty of _ thy _ peace, The

- ter - pre - ted by love! Drop through the heats _ of _ our de - sire Thy
beau - ty of thy peace. Breathe

cool - ness and thy balm; Let sense be dumb, let flesh re - tire; Speak through the earth - quake,

wind and _ fire, O _ still small voice _ of _ calm, O still small voice of calm.

Moving on

fact file
Can you see the change of key at bar 37? When music change
key in the middle of a piece it is called a **modulation**.

Pam Wedgwoo

Further support and information

Now you are on your way, there are already lots of opportunities for using your new-found skills. But to progress further you should find a suitable singing teacher close to you. Organisations that can help in your search include:

- **AOTOS** (Association of Teachers of Singing) www.aotos.org.uk
  Tel: 01934 412921
- **ISM** (Incorporated Society of Musicians) www.ism.org
  Tel: 0207 629 4413
- **Musicians Union** www.musiciansunion.org.uk
  Tel: 0207 582 5566

Most teachers will give you a consultation lesson which is an opportunity for you to try them out and see if you would like to work with them and vice versa. It is important that the teacher/pupil relationship is right, so be prepared to search out the best person for you.

Thinking of joining a choir?

You may think a choir is the right direction for you. There are all sorts of different choirs – choral societies, barbershop choirs, ladies choirs, church choirs and close harmony groups to name but a few. Go along and hear some local groups perform – look out for concerts in your area and see if you like the music they sing. Some choirs may require you to do an audition, others don't. Some choirs ask you to come to a few rehearsals before you join, but the choir secretary will give you all this information when you apply. Choral singing is a fantastic way of meeting new friends, performing in amazing buildings and even travelling to exotic locations.

Want to get on stage?

If you really enjoy acting, then you may like to think about joining an amateur dramatic society or a Gilbert and Sullivan society. If you've never acted before then volunteer to help back stage first to get an idea of what is involved. Keep an eye out on community noticeboards and local newspapers as many amateur groups advertise at the start of a new production. Most societies will have their own web sites but here are a few generic ones which might help you:

- www.amdram.co.uk
- www.amateurdramatic.co.uk

Getting competitive

Finally, there are hundreds of amateur singing competitions that you can enter, but it is probably best to have the support of a singing teacher behind you so that you are prepared well. Used carefully, they can be a useful tool in improving your overall performance, but if you enter too soon they can knock your confidence. A teacher will know when you are ready for a competition, so follow their advice.

- www.federationoffestivals.org.uk

Contents